ESSAY PEASY

HOW TO WRITE ANY GCSE ESSAY WITH EASE!

DARREN COXON

Life isn't always easy peasy, but my family always make it worthwhile.

CONTENTS

✳ Created with Vellum

WELCOME!

THIS BOOK FORMS PART OF the Examiner's Head series of GCSE, A-Level and IB revision guides. The series takes you inside the dark and mysterious world of the examiner's head, working out just how to get marks with every single thing you write. By thinking like an examiner, you're far more likely to tick their boxes, and the more ticks you receive the higher your grade!

Other books in the series:

AQA English Language IGCSE 9-1

Macbeth for AQA GCSE

An Inspector Calls for GCSE

Darren Coxon has been teaching English for a very long time. He's put countless hundreds of students successfully through GCSE, A-Level and IB exams. He credits his success with a tried and tested formula refined over many years, which focuses in on exactly the skills and knowledge that examiners are looking to assess.

Darren is currently Director of Schools for a UK schools group. He lives in Harrogate with his wife, two children and one Siamese cat. When he's not writing he loves to run, play guitar and cook.

WHAT'S THE POINT OF ESSAYS?

I've been in education for around 25 years, and teaching for more than 20. In that time, I've come to understand the importance of the 'why'.

Why do you need to learn to write essays? What's the point of learning to write argument, analysis or description? Why on earth should you care about writing stories?

You may be mathematical and laser focused on doing maths and science at A-Level or IB. So why do you have to go through the torture of writing about a novel, poem or passage you'll never have to look at again?

Some might say 'you need to learn to write in order to pass exams'. And to some extent that's true. But it's such a tiny part of why the techniques I'm going to teach you are so important for your future success.

I cannot stress to you enough how important communication is nowadays. People who can communicate well are at a huge advantage. There are so many competing voices, so much noise out there. You have to be the one with the clear voice who can cut through all that.

So, learning to write logical, intelligent and well thought-through essays is critical. True, you may never need to write another argument essay about capital punishment again, but I can guarantee you that at some point in your future careers you're going to have to present your point of view and make others agree with you.

Or take information, summarise it and write your opinion on it. Perhaps even write creatively if your career revolves around convincing others through a well told narrative.

Use the ideas in this book, practise as much as you can, ace your exams, and be successful!

I hope this book helps: do leave me a review at the end if so!

QUILBOT IS NOT YOUR FRIEND

Please, please, for the love of all things loveable, don't use Quilbot.

Or Word AI, Article Spinner, Rewriting AI, or any of the other websites that use machine intelligence to rewrite an essay you've copied from the internet to try and fool your teacher.

Because guess what?

They don't work. None of them. So don't bother.

Most of you will have been in the position where time has run out and that critical piece of coursework hasn't been done. Maybe you weren't inspired by the title, or had too much on, or procrastinated as there was always something more interesting to do.

Perhaps you've also Googled 'mice and men essay' (insert title to suit), copied what you found, pasted it into Quilbot and hey presto! An essay similar to the one you just copied but also different. As good as an essay you'd written yourself!

Only it wasn't. Not even close.

You see, over time your teacher gets to know your writing style. Your vocabulary, how you structure sentences and so on. As soon as you stray off that well-trodden path you're in trouble, and no amount of artificial 'intelligence' will help you.

It'd be a bit like lining up at the start of a 100 metre race on a motorbike. People might notice that you're attempting an unfair advantage.

What teachers do, if they're suspicious, is copy a paragraph of your essay into Google or one of a number of plagiarism detectors to see what comes up. And even if you've run 'your' essay a few times through one of these online word manglers there will be enough similar to confirm the teacher's suspicions.

Plagiarism is serious. I have known of students who have been kicked off an entire course for doing exactly what I've outlined above. It's not worth it.

The other crazy thing about cheating is that you'll have exams where it's just you and a piece of paper in a drafty hall with a boy sniffing annoyingly behind you as he forgot to bring tissues into the exam room. And guess what? You don't have Quilbot. No machine can help you now. You're on your own.

So, stop right there. The fact you're reading this means you know that Quilbot is not your friend. Perhaps you tried it once, perhaps you got away with it. But I bet you felt hollow inside, didn't you? Just a tiny bit.

It's far better to apply a few simple rules to your preparation and a clear, repeatable structure to your writing, as it's genuinely rewarding to craft an essay that fluently translates onto paper what's inside your head.

Without further ado, let's get started!

THE FOUR DIFFERENT TYPES OF ESSAY

I'm sure that the reason you're reading this guide is because you're stuck. You've an essay to write and cannot get away from the blank page. You have ideas but you don't know where to start.

That's totally normal. No one can write an essay, whether it's persuasive, descriptive or whatever, without learning the ingredients first. It's the same as learning to bake a cake. You have flour and eggs and whatnot, but someone needs to tell you how much of everything to put in, and how long to bake it for.

With an essay, you have words and sentences and paragraphs, but which words, what sort of sentences, what length of paragraph?

This book will take you through the four main types of essay that you'll encounter in your exams:

- Persuasive/Argumentative (sometimes called Discursive)
- Descriptive
- Narrative
- Analytical/Explanatory

I'll talk you through each one in turn, showing you how to plan, structure and write. I'll focus on the ingredients of each essay type, so that when you're under pressure you can fall back on a simple, repeatable recipe. Just like baking a cake (I love cake).

Let's look briefly at the four types of essay:

1. PERSUASIVE/ARGUMENTATIVE/DISCURSIVE

This will take different points of view on a subject, present them logically, and make clear why one particular point of view is the one the reader should take.

In many ways it's the most personal of all the essay forms but it's also the one that is easy to fall down on as it needs careful structuring. You'll hear it referred to as either a **persuasive** essay (as you're trying to persuade someone to think like you), **argument** (as you are arguing one point of view) or **discursive** (as you're discussing a subject, looking at both points of view).

The tricks you'll learn when writing persuasively can be used for public speaking as well. There is little difference between an argument essay and a debate.

2. DESCRIPTIVE

This is the one that has the most chance of being dull and switching your audience off. You might be asked to describe waking up on a tropical island, or the sights and sounds at rush hour where you live. Either one of these has the potential to be a car crash (no apology for the traffic-related pun). Writing descriptively is all about detail - the smaller the better. It's also about using all your senses, not just your sight.

3. NARRATIVE

AKA writing a story. You could say this isn't really an essay, but as this book is all about preparing you for all of the different types of writing you're likely to come across in your exam, it makes sense to include it here. You'll have narrative questions in your Language exam, and some Literature exams ask you write from the point of view of a character (known as transformational writing).

4. ANALYTICAL

This is the most common essay type when you're studying Literature GCSE and A-Level/IB. It's the 'how do the quotes answer the question' type of essay. And it's likely to be the one you find hardest. Not surprising as guess what! It is the hardest. So don't worry if analysis stresses you out. Hopefully by the end of this book it won't seem quite so daunting.

———

I'll now take you through each of these types of essay, breaking them down into their component parts, and then give you plenty of opportunity to practise. Each section will also look at different exam board questions to show you how you might approach tackling them.

And no Examiner's Head book would be complete without showing you how Assessment Objectives are your friends. I'll look at those as well.

If you've stumbled on this looking for a more advanced book for A Level and IB essay writing, then what I talk through within is as relevant to you as to GCSE students. Analysing is always the same, whether it's writing about a short passage or a whole novel. The difference is the depth to which you dig.

Let's turn first of all to writing persuasively.

1

WRITING PERSUASIVELY

persuasion

/pəˈsweɪʒ(ə)n/

noun

noun: **persuasion**; plural noun: **persuasions**

the action or process of persuading someone or of being persuaded to do or believe something.

When writing persuasively, you want your reader to either *do* or *believe* something by the time they have finished your essay. *Doing* might be persuading people to recycle, and *believing* might be believing in God or Santa Claus (not that anyone needs to be persuaded of Santa's existence).

I'm starting with persuasive essays as their structure is fairly easy to understand. Plus, in an exam, providing you follow the rules I outline below, it doesn't matter whether you know anything about the subject, or believe what you are writing. You'll get good marks.

You may hear teachers refer to these essays as either Argument or Discursive. They're all the same. You are *discussing* a topic, are *arguing* for one side or the other, and trying to *persuade* the reader. So don't worry if your teacher uses a different term.

Let's go through the rules first, before we apply them to an exam-style question.

THE 5 RULES OF WRITING PERSUASIVELY

1. Choose a position

This means decide which **point of view** you're going to be persuasive/argue from. It doesn't have to be what you believe and you don't have to care about the subject (although it helps to have some opinion either way as it can make your writing more passionate).

Often the question will ask you take a point of view either for or against, but sometimes it doesn't so it's important to decide from the start which viewpoint you will take.

For example, let's say you're going to try and persuade someone to recycle. You begin all your planning with that position in mind, not undecided yourself.

The reason this is important will become clearer in a moment, when we come to the research stage.

2. Know who you're writing for

If you're writing an exam or coursework essay, the actual audience is your teacher or examiner, but many questions will tell you the audience you are supposedly writing for. Take this example:

> Write a letter to your local member of parliament explaining why you think your town should improve its recycling.

On this occasion, you're writing to an MP so your writing will be formal. It will be very different to this example:

> Write an email to your classmates persuading them of the importance of recycling.

We will think more about this later.

3. Do the research

In order to be convincing you need facts, statistics, evidence and examples to illustrate your point of view.

For a coursework essay this is the most interesting part of the planning process, as you can amaze/bore your friends and family with all the interesting information you learn about climate change or why music is important for our mental health.

But, I hear you cry! How can I research in an exam? Don't worry: in an exam it's not about what you know about the subject. You're being examined on how well you use the right language, structure and techniques to present a convincing argument. So you can add facts and data that you make up. (Within reason, of course: it needs to sound believable.)

Important point: when you're researching, you're finding evidence both **for** and **against** your point of view. Don't just look for evidence to support the viewpoint you are arguing from. This is what we call **confirmation bias**: in other words, only looking for evidence which **confirms** your point of view. You want the reader to consider the other side before you explain to them that this is wrong.

Say you want to argue that studying arts subjects at school (like music and art) is as important as English and Maths. Maybe you find some online article that suggests that every employer wants employees with really good Maths. You can then find an article with a **counter** (opposite) argument which says that being creative is as important as being mathematical nowadays. And then explain why you don't agree with it.

I'll give you more ideas when we look at some exam type questions below.

4. Pick out the most important and most convincing evidence

You've done your research and found a pile of different examples to back up your point of view and counter/oppose the other point of view.

But how do you work out which are important and which aren't? Choose 4-5 of the strongest and most emotive. That would make the reader think 'yes, you're right, I'm on your side'. The more attention-grabbing the evidence, the better.

For example, for recycling you want evidence that shows the terrible cost to the environment due to plastic waste being dumped at sea or those massive rubbish dumps we see in developing countries. If it's about humans or animals suffering then it's sure to make people take notice.

I'm not trying to be cynical about this at all: but your job is to make the examiner (or your teacher) sits up and takes notice. So make it attention-grabbing wherever possible, whatever you actually believe. It's honestly ok if you don't hugely care about either side: it's all about following the rules and presenting a logical and thoughtful argument.

Again, as you do this, make sure you pick out the main points from the other point of view as you're going to use these to write your counter (opposing) argument.

More on all this when we turn to our real world example.

5. The Seven Ps

Seven Ps?

There's an old military saying, which is as good for life as it is for essays:

Proper Planning and Preparation Prevents Piss Poor Performance.

You'll remember that one because of the word that stands out.

I'm not a naturally good planner. When I write my books, I have an outline but much of it is quite organic. The difference between me and you (and no, it's not just the age) is that I have an awful lot of experience as a writer, and I don't have the sort of time pressure that you'll have in an exam.

Planning, therefore, is pretty important. Even if it's just five minutes at the start, mapping out your arguments and paragraphs is useful as it can help to organise your thoughts.

PUTTING IT INTO PRACTICE

Let's look at how we might tackle this in an exam. We can look at the AQA November 2018 Writing question 5 as it's a good example of what I've been talking through above:

> 5. 'Cars are noisy, dirty, smelly and downright dangerous. They should be banned from all town and city centres, allowing people to walk and cycle in peace.'
>
> Write a letter to the Minister for Transport arguing your point of view on this statement.
>
> (24 marks for content and organisation 16 marks for technical accuracy) **[40 marks]**
>
> You are advised to plan your answer to Question 5 before you start to write.

When you see a phrase like 'you are advised' it is the examiner's way of saying 'please please please at least do a little bit of planning so I don't have to read yet another pile of vomit on the page'. Trust me, I've read enough bad essays to know just how it makes teachers and examiners feel.

It's worth turning our attention briefly to the Assessment Objectives for this question. Think of AOs like a tick list, nothing more. Every single thing you write should tick off an AO. This is how you get top marks.

AO5

Communicate clearly, effectively and imaginatively, selecting and adapting tone, style and register for different forms, purposes and audiences.

Organise information and ideas, using structural and grammatical features to support coherence and cohesion of texts.

AO6

Candidates must use a range of vocabulary and sentence structures for clarity, purpose and effect, with accurate spelling and punctuation. (This requirement must constitute 20% of the marks for each specification as a whole).

In other words:

- Make sure you write clearly
- Make sure your style matches who you're writing to
- Make sure you use punctuation and paragraphs
- Make sure you use a wide vocabulary

STRUCTURING YOUR ARGUMENT/PERSUASION ESSAY

I'm sure you'll have been taught this, but it's always good to remind ourselves as if you get this right you should be on your way to a very good essay. Each of the numbers represents a paragraph:

1. **Introduction**. This will open with an attention grabbing sentence, give an overview of the argument, and state your point of view. Nothing more.
2. **Body paragraph 1**: evidence and explanation for your side of the argument.
3. **Body paragraph 2**: further evidence for your side of the argument.
4. **Body paragraph 3**: even more evidence for your side of the argument.
5. **Body paragraph 4**: evidence from the other point of view, but ones you effectively argue against.

6. **Conclusion**: summarise your main points and close with a powerful sentence.

Numbers 2-5 aren't set in stone: you might alternate one paragraph for and one against, or have two paragraphs for then one against. The most important thing is that each paragraph will explore one reason either for or against your point of view.

GOOD IDEA...

If the question gives you the option of taking either side, think about which side of the argument most people in the exam will argue from… and then do the opposite. In this case, most people will argue that yes, cars are smelly and dirty etc, but you're going to say that they **shouldn't** be banned from city centres. Doesn't matter if this isn't what you actually think, as to be honest the exam marker doesn't care about your point of view, just whether you can write a convincing argument.

STEP BY STEP FROM PLANNING TO WRITING

Let's take the question above and think about exactly how we'd approach it. I'll give you some other examples to practise a bit later.

5. 'Cars are noisy, dirty, smelly and downright dangerous. They should be banned from all town and city centres, allowing people to walk and cycle in peace.'

Write a letter to the Minister for Transport arguing your point of view on this statement.

(24 marks for content and organisation 16 marks for technical accuracy) **[40 marks]**

You are advised to plan your answer to Question 5 before you start to write.

1. The first thing you'll want to do is decide on **which point**

of view you will argue from. As I suggest above, I'm going to argue **against** the statement, saying that it's important *not* to ban cars from town and city centres (I like a challenge).

2. You're now going to brainstorm all the reasons why you think you **shouldn't** ban cars. This should take you no more than 5 minutes. These are the ones I can think of:

3. *If cars are banned people will shop in out of town shopping centres and city centre shops will close, turning cities into ghosts towns.*

4. *It should be everyone's choice to decide on how they get around - government shouldn't dictate what transport we use and act like parents.*

5. *Old people often struggle with buses - getting on and off etc. Cars give them a lifeline which if they are removed can leave old people feeling isolated and lonely.*

6. *Cars are getting greener and greener, with more people buying electric cars like Teslas so the pollution argument will soon die out.*

7. *More buses often means more pollution.*

8. *Those big bendy buses are more dangerous to cyclists than cars.*

9. Let's now think about the arguments for the statement, that it would be better for cars **not** to be in city centres:

10. Safer for pedestrians and cyclists

11. Better for the environment

12. People are more likely to walk further or cycle so better for health

13. You are then going to make a note of your arguments against these points. This is important if you want to get more than a Grade 5. A quick exercise like the below is useful. Examiners will also see this in your planning which will help to demonstrate that you have actually *planned*. The **counter argument** means the argument **against**: in other words, how you're going to explain that the other point of view is just plain wrong...

14. **For**: Safer for pedestrians and cyclists

15. **Counter Argument**: Buses are more dangerous, people walking into town having to cross busy roads

16. **For**: Better for the environment

17. **Counter argument**: Buses pollute, cars are getting greener
18. **For**: Better for health
19. **Counter argument**: Car parks often not in the centre of town so people have to walk, bus stops usually are in centre of town so walk less

GOOD IDEA..

Before we start, here are a few extra tips to help you stand out from the crowd (and it's a pretty big crowd, remember, as the exam marker will probably be wading through 500 of these essays. I know! But they do get paid.)

1. Make it **personal**: the pronouns 'I', 'you' and 'we' will make the reader feel a connection with the writer's point of view.
2. Bring in **facts and statistics** (even if it's an exam and you've made them up) - saying things like 'in a recent survey, 70% of respondents said that their next car would be electric' gives your argument weight as it shows you've done your research. If it's coursework, do make sure you actually research…
3. Use **connectives** to help your essay flow. Examples include
4. 'On the one hand…. On the other hand….'
5. 'Some say that… however, others argue…'
6. 'It could be argued that…. However,…'
7. 'It is clear that….'
8. 'It is obvious that…'
9. 'It is incorrect to say that…'
10. 'One could argue that…'
11. 'Firstly…. Secondly…. Finally…'
12. 'Furthermore…'
13. 'Moreover…'
14. 'Conversely…'

15. Ask **rhetorical questions** (ones that don't need an answer as they're obvious). These can be very powerful.
16. 'Would you like it if...?'
17. 'Is that what our world wants/deserves/needs?'
18. 'Do you really want this to happen?'
19. 'Can you imagine a world where....?'
20. Use **emotive words** (words that generate emotions in the reader), both positive (for your side of the argument) and negative (against the other side). We'll see these in action below.
21. Use the **rule of three** to get your point across: 'I am shocked, appalled and saddened by...'.

THE ESSAY

Drum roll... The moment you've been waiting for. Let's see all this in action. You may want to have a go at writing your own version before reading the one below. It's up to you. There are plenty of additional questions at the end of this chapter for you to practise.

Let's start with the **introduction** and then think about how it works:

Dear Minister,

I am sure that you receive countless letters from teenagers like myself, asking you to banish cars from our city centres. They tend to argue that cars are filthy, polluting and dangerous, and that only by removing them totally from our towns and cities can we hope to live healthier and safer lives. However, I would like to argue the opposite, that cars are in fact an important factor in keeping our towns alive. I ask that you take my points into consideration when making your decision.

Key points:

1. First off, look at the opening sentence. Now that is an attention grabber. You know why? Even though the letter is

addressed to the Minister, the exam marker will indeed have read countless letters arguing that cars should be banned. So he or she is probably feeling a bit jaded about the whole thing. It's quite a clever way of hooking the *actual* audience (exam marker) in.

2. The tone is formal from the first sentence: small details such as using 'I am' rather than 'I'm', 'receive' rather than 'get', and 'countless' rather than 'lots'. If you make those changes it sounds totally different: 'I'm sure you get lots of letters…'

3. This letter begins with the other side of the argument: 'They tend to argue that…'. It then brings in the writer's point of view being argued, using the connective 'However,…'. This is the best way to move from one side of the argument to the other.

4. There are emotive words dotted around: 'banish' is a dramatic word, as are 'filthy, polluting and dangerous'. However, rather than being used to back up the writer's point of view, they are being used in a deliberately over the top way, to make the other argument seem melodramatic. If you can make the other side sound over emotional you have more chance to come across as being balanced and intelligent. Politicians do this all the time.

5. The introduction ends with an appeal to the reader: 'I ask that you…' This is a very powerful technique as it's basically saying 'look, hear me out, I'll convince you'. It positions the reader to take the writer's points into consideration, even if they actually believe the opposite to be true.

6. Look at how short it is: you don't need a huge intro paragraph. In fact, most of your paragraphs should be no more than 3-4 sentences in length. It's much easier for an examiner to read the essay if the paragraphs are short.

The Main Body

Let's move on to the **main body** of the essay.

Our cities are in crisis. Shops closing every week, people losing their jobs, row after row of graffitied, boarded up shop fronts where there once was hustle and bustle. Do you want that to happen? Well, by banning cars from our city centres this is exactly what will be the result. In the last 15 years there has been a 50% drop in the number of people going into towns to shop: they prefer out of town shopping centres and online ordering. Do you think that removing cars from cities will help? Of course not: if people have to rely on buses to get into town they are far more likely to head to the out of town mall. Removing cars will destroy our centres.

This paragraph ticks every box for a top grade:

1. A punchy opening sentence. Short and attention grabbing.
2. Lots of emotive words: 'crisis', 'row after row', 'destroy'.
3. The rule of three: shops closing, people losing jobs, boarded up shops.
4. Rhetorical questions the reader cannot help but answer in their head: 'Do you want that to happen?'
5. Use of statistics: '15 years', '50% drop'.
6. Use of colons to introduce the opinion then back it up: 'Of course not:…'
7. Another punchy closing sentence to sum up the main point in the paragraph.

The Next Point

We can then move the essay on to the next point.

It is not easy getting old. You slow down, you can't walk as far as you used to, and you can feel more and more isolated. If cars are banned from our cities then the more elderly drivers will no longer be able to go into town to meet their friends or shop. They don't want to go to some faceless out of town mall with its enormous car park they can never find their car in: they want the comfort and familiarity of the town. Some might say that the elderly are better off using buses, but what if they need to carry home heavy shopping? Surely it is easier for them to have their car near the shops than have to walk a distance from the bus stop to home. By removing cars from our towns, you will be removing the elderly's lifeline to the outside world.

I think you're starting to get the idea. Can you see how different this is to the majority of persuasive essays? It is being creative, passionate, emotive, occasionally even a little angry. That's what will grab the exam marker's attention and that's what will get you the decent grades.

Another technique used in this paragraph is the 'what if' question. That's a good way of showing the consequence of the other side's point of view.

The Counter Argument

Let's look now at a paragraph which gives an argument against, and how you might counter it.

One of the principal arguments in favour of banning cars from towns is the impact it will have on the environment. Cars emit high volumes of carbon monoxide which has been proven to impact on global warming. But more and more car owners are turning to hybrid or electric cars. In the last year alone, sales of electric cars have more than tripled, and by 2030 the current government wishes to ban the sale of all petrol and diesel cars. And whilst some buses are greener than others, the fact remains that most still belch out horrific diesel fumes that are far more polluting than the average modern car. Is it really such a good idea to fill our streets with these polluting monsters? Surely it is better to allow cars to continue to drive into towns, safe in the knowledge that, day by day, they are getting kinder to the environment.

The paragraph begins by stating the counter/opposing argument - that cars are bad for the environment. What it then does is take the main point of that argument and effectively demonstrate that this is increasingly not the case (bringing in some statistics ('more than tripled') to back up the point). It then brings in the alternative (buses) and suggests they are not very green.

The examiner isn't going to care whether that is 100% true or not, as you are not being marked on your knowledge of car versus bus exhaust emissions (have a look back at the Assessment Objectives if you don't believe me). You are being marked on h**ow effectively you structure your argument and the techniques you use**.

The Conclusion

If this was an exam you'd not be expected to write any more than 3 main body paragraphs as you won't have time. So, let's move on to the conclusion.

> As you can see, banning cars from towns is not the answer. It will rob struggling businesses of much needed revenue, further turning our much loved city centres into ghost towns. It will isolate our elderly who often rely on their cars to access shops and social spaces. And it isn't going to save the environment as cars are getting greener every day, unlike the majority of buses. I urge you not to listen to the voices that only see one side of the story, and instead consider whether destroying our towns and cities is worth it. I hope you realise that it is not.

You want to save some of the most emotive, impactful language to the conclusion, as you want to make sure you leave the reader in no doubt that your point of view is the one worth considering.

The main technique it uses is to **already assume the reader is on the writer's side**. By beginning 'As you can see' it immediately suggests that there is only one point of view worth considering. This is a technique politicians use all the time.

From there, it goes through each of the main points in the essay, one sentence per point. It then makes a plea to the reader ('I urge you') to take the writer's side, before ending on a final, firm and clear, statement: 'I hope you realise that it is not.'

Putting it all together

OK, let's put it all together into one and we can see how it reads:

Dear Minister,

I am sure that you receive countless letters from teenagers like myself, asking you to banish cars from our city centres. They tend to argue that cars are filthy, polluting and dangerous, and that only by removing them totally from our towns and cities can we hope to live healthier and safer lives. However, I would like to argue the opposite, that cars are in fact an important factor in keeping our towns alive. I ask that you take my points into consideration when making your decision.

Our cities are in crisis. Shops closing every week, people losing their jobs, row after row of graffitied, boarded up shop fronts where there once was hustle and bustle. Do you want that to happen? Well, by banning cars from our city centres this is exactly what will be the result. In the last 15 years there has been a 50% drop in the number of people going into towns to shop: they prefer out of town shopping centres and online ordering. Do you think that removing cars from cities will help? Of course not: if people have to rely on buses to get into town they are far more likely to head to the out of town mall. Removing cars will destroy our centres.

It is not easy getting old. You slow down, you can't walk as far as you used to, and you can feel more and more isolated. If cars are banned from our cities then the more elderly drivers will no longer be able to go into town to meet their friends or shop. They don't want to go to some faceless out of town mall with its enormous car park they can never find their car in: they want the comfort and familiarity of the town. Some might say that the elderly are better off using buses, but what if they need to carry home heavy shopping? Surely it is easier for them to have their car near the shops than have to walk a distance from the bus stop to home. By removing cars from our towns, you will be removing the elderly's lifeline to the outside world.

One of the principal arguments in favour of banning cars from towns is the impact it will have on the environment. Cars emit high volumes of carbon monoxide which has been proven to impact on global warming. But more and more car owners are turning to hybrid or electric cars. In the last year alone, sales of electric cars have more than tripled, and by 2030 the current government wishes to ban the sale of all petrol and diesel cars. And whilst some buses are greener than others, the fact remains that most still belch out horrific diesel fumes that are far more polluting than the average modern car. Is it really such a good idea to fill our streets with these polluting monsters? Surely it is better to allow cars to continue to drive into towns, safe in the knowledge that, day by day, they are getting kinder to the environment.

As you can see, banning cars from towns is not the answer. It will rob struggling businesses of much needed revenue, further turning our much loved city centres into ghost towns. It will isolate our elderly who often rely on their cars to access shops and social spaces. And it isn't going to save the environment as cars are getting greener every day, unlike the majority of buses. I urge you not to listen to the voices that only see one side of the story, and instead consider whether destroying our towns and cities is worth it. I hope you realise that it is not.

Yours sincerely,

A. Person

Pretty persuasive, don't you think? By following a strict structure, and making sure you tick off all the AOs, you'll get high marks. **Remember: this question is not examining you on your subject knowledge**. You can make statistics up, provided you do so in a way that adds to the power of the argument and doesn't look silly: for example, if you said above that scientists have proven the world will end if cars are banned from towns, the examiner might raise their eyebrows (in the way I'm sure you've seen teachers do).

OVER TO YOU

Here are some questions for you to practise. Follow the exact same method as above - don't miss a step. You can also use the same structure when you write your essay.

1. The world would be a happier and better place if cars / tobacco / television / computers, etc. (you choose a topic) had never existed. Write the text of a speech to your year group in which you argue either for or against this proposition.
2. The disciplining of children by smacking is often in the news. Write an article for your school magazine arguing for or against smacking by parents.
3. Write a blog article in which you argue whether dogs are better than cats.

That's the first essay in the bag. I hope you have seen that it's really not too tricky so long as you follow the rules.

Let's now turn to writing descriptively.

(2)

WRITING DESCRIPTIVELY

description

/dɪˈskrɪpʃ(ə)n/

noun

noun: **description**; plural noun: **descriptions**

1. a spoken or written account of a person, object, or event.

To describe is to take what is in your mind and communicate it in such a way as to make the reader or listener see what you're seeing, hear what you're hearing, feel what you're feeling. It is the most powerful of written forms but can really trip you up if you get it wrong.

Why? Because, without knowing exactly how to prepare for a descriptive question, your writing is likely to be boring.

And I mean *really* boring.

Don't take it personally. Writing tedious description doesn't make *you* boring. One doesn't follow the other. You just need to follow a few rules. Let's look at them first.

1. Descriptive writing is all about detail

I cannot stress enough how important details are when you are describing. Let me illustrate this for you.

Say you were the victim of a robbery. Someone ran past you and grabbed your phone. You chased them and as they were running they tripped and you got a brief look at their face. When you sit with the police artist (whose job it is to take a victim's description and turn it into a drawing) they will ask you specific questions. Not just hair colour but shape of face, whether eyes slanted downwards, thin or thick lips and so on.

The problem, of course, is that you only saw them briefly, so your description is bound to be limited. So what the artist comes up with looks nothing like the man who robbed you.

It's the same with writing to describe. Unless you make it specific what you're describing then the reader hasn't a clue. Don't just say 'some people stood waiting', say 'three men stood waiting, one tall, two shorter. All wore the traditional uniform.' Think of it like adding detail to a painting: it's the difference between a stick figure and the Mona Lisa.

2. It's as much about what you don't say, as what you say

It may seem that this point contradicts number 1 above. If you need lots of detail, surely you don't leave anything out? Not quite. Whilst you should focus on small details, they're the details you want to draw the reader's attention to.

Say you're describing a photograph of a railway station at rush hour. Imagine trying to describe every tiny thing in that scene in minute detail. You'd not get past describing the platform with every piece of litter and chewing gum and the colour of the pigeon's feathers.

(There's a famous book by a writer called James Joyce, who describes one day in the life of a young man called Stephen Dedalus. It's called *Ulysses*, is more than 700 pages long, and is almost impossible to read. Don't believe me? Download the first section from Amazon.)

What you want to do is imagine you're a film director. Where are you going to train your camera? Will it be a long shot, or close up? Will you start wide and zoom in, which is what most directors would do?

3. Description should be subjective

What do I mean? Well, who is doing the describing? Is it some emotionless robot, a sort of descriptive Quilbot, doing the writing? No, it's you! And you are person, with your own feelings and emotions and reactions and so on.

When you describe, you do so from your point of view (or the point of view of the character if it's a work of fiction). It is rare to have totally objective (not personal) description. The very fact you are taking what's in your head and writing it down is personal. They are your words. These are your choices as to what to show and what not to show.

4. It's not just what you see

But also what you hear, taste, touch and smell. If you want to place the reader in the scene you're describing then you need to use more than one sense. You don't have to use them all, but bringing in what you hear and smell as well as what you see can be powerful.

HOW TO PLAN FOR THE TOP GRADES

You might think that writing description is just about sitting in the exam room, staring into space and waiting for inspiration to visit you. Perhaps you hope for a moment of awakening, where after a few minutes' meditation your pen springs to life (like Mickey Mouse's broom in *Fantasia*) and the descriptive passage sort of writes itself.

If only.

Nope, you need to do a bit of planning first. Like writing a persuasive/argument essay, those few minutes getting a few details down will be invaluable when you come to writing.

A sample question

Let's say the question shows you a photo of a busy train station at rush hour. Light is streaming in through three large windows at the end of the station concourse. The question is:

'Using the image below, describe a morning at rush hour when you are late for work.'

Taking initial notes

Here is my fool proof way to blast down a few notes and ideas to get you thinking about what to focus on before you begin to write your answer.

1. Begin by writing down **5 things you see** in the photo. Try to include adjectives so it's clear what you're listing. They should be the first things you notice as these are the most important details. Be super specific here - try to describe using concrete details.
2. If you can, add **3 similes or metaphors** that are suggested (such as cathedral-like windows).
3. Write down **3 things you might hear** were you in the scene.
4. Write down **1-2 things you might smell**. Don't worry about how to describe them, just what you smell (like burgers or coffee).
5. Make a note of 1-2 textures you might touch
6. Make a note of what **mood** the photo conjures up (happy? sad? mysterious? threatening?)
7. Finally, make a note of the **emotions** you would experience were you there and late for work.

Do this now, then compare your list with what I've noted down.

My list

- Reflections of people walking fast on the shiny floor
- Three cathedral-like windows
- Domed arches above like a church
- People look like beetles scurrying along
- Light pooled on the floor from the windows
- Buzzing noise of constant movement
- Tannoy announcing the next train
- Baby crying
- Croissant smell
- Metallic smell you always get at railway stations
- Cool metallic turnstile
- Smooth ticket in your hand
- Mood - restless, busy, energetic
- Emotions - stressed, anxious, not really able to take in the beauty of the building

Next up, look back at the list and see if you can add any more specific details - for example, can you think of a more interesting way of describing the smell of the croissants? Maybe 'buttery, fresh, warm smell of morning croissants'.

8 TIPS FOR EXCELLENT DESCRIPTIVE WRITING

Here are 8 tips that should help you before you put pen to paper.

1. Think about from which **point of view** the majority of people in the exam will write this description. Correct, first person: 'I saw….I heard….I smelt..' But you're not going to do that, are you? Because you want your essay to be the one that stands out and has your teacher or the exam marker thinking 'finally, a candidate with some originality.' So, you're going to write in either the third person 'he/she' or, even more originally, the second person 'you'. What, I hear you cry? Write in the second person? I think this is a

brilliant way to write description. Let me show you what I mean.

2. Take this sentence: 'I looked up and saw the vaulted arches of the station and the cathedral-like windows, light pouring onto the floor below. I walked across the concourse, my senses alive to the changing scents as I passed by burger stalls and coffee shops.'

3. Now see how it reads in the second person: 'You look up and see the vaulted arches of the station and the cathedral-like windows, light pouring onto the floor below. You walk across the concourse, your senses alive to the changing scents as you pass by burger stalls and coffee shops.'

4. Quite effective, isn't it? The reason is that it is forcing the reader to imagine they are there. Because you are telling them they are! Clever, eh…. You can pay me later (oh, you have already as you bought this book).

5. Did you notice what else I did in the above switch from first to second? That's right, I switched from **past tense to present tense**. Again, I think this is a more effective tense to use for description as it places the reader there at that moment, rather than looking back as a memory.

6. Make sure you use the **active form of the verb**, not the passive. Passive voice kills description. By active, I mean using 'you see', 'you hear', 'you notice' rather than 'you have seen', 'you have heard' and 'you have noticed'. You generally want to avoid the passive voice in your writing as it adds more words than are necessary and can draw the reader away from the scene.

7. Remember: it's all about **detail**. So, when you describe something, try to be as specific as possible. Don't just say 'you smell burgers cooking' but rather 'you smell the oily, rich and slightly sweet scent of burgers cooking'.

8. Think about the **techniques** you'll have been taught when writing about poetry, and use some of them in your description. In fact, the more poetic you make this piece of writing, the better. Simile, metaphor, alliteration, consonance, assonance (I've listed definitions in the back of

the book). I used one above - did you see the sibilance in the burger description? (Sibilance is the repetition of the 's' sound - a form of alliteration.)

WHAT NOT TO DO

You've made your notes, tried to add a bit more detail and thrown in a few similes for good measure. Now, how do you actually start the answer?

There is no 100% correct way to begin (sometimes I wish I was a maths teacher - their lives are so much easier. Yes or no, right or wrong, tick or cross. Oh well *sighs*). However, there are a few wrong ways.

Don't do the below if you want a decent grade:

- Begin with something like 'I was walking across the station and I saw some people walking quickly and some pigeons flew overhead.'
- Or maybe start with this classic: 'I look across the station and see shops selling ice cream and sandwiches.'
- Or perhaps: 'It was very noisy in the station. There was a lot of movement. It seemed like everyone needed to be somewhere else.'

What is wrong with these? They are all grammatically correct. But that's where the positives end:

- passive voice ('I was walking')
- vagueness ('some')
- stating the obvious ('I look', 'I see')
- boring ('shops selling ice cream')
- cliched and obvious ('seemed like everyone needed to be somewhere else' - er yes, that's because they do. As they are in a train station.)

WHAT TO DO

Ok, I hear you say. Smart Alec, telling me all the wrong ways to do it. But what about how to do it properly?

I'm coming to that. Be patient! All will be revealed.

Let's look at a sample opening then think about how it ticks the boxes to get the top grade:

Light streams in from the cathedral-like windows at the end of the concourse, catching the dust that hangs in the air and reflecting back from the polished marble floor. You stand at the entrance, caught suddenly by the restless movement and frantic energy that buzzes around you. People like beetles, caught black against the sharp sunlight; silhouettes, moving, moving, left and right, towards you and away from you, never stopping. Always somewhere else to go, the station having no purpose other than to funnel people to their next destination.

You walk across the concourse, pulling your case behind you, wheels whirring on the smooth surface. All around is the noise of the tannoy: 'the next train to depart from…. calling at….' None of the place names matter to you: you know where you are going. The sharp metallic twang, that unmistakeable scent of station, is suddenly replaced by the warm comfort of baked goods: croissants and baguettes baked to order at the Greggs next to platform nine. You keep moving, attempting to ignore the sudden hunger pangs. You don't have time to stop. You never have time.

You can probably see how that might get you a very good mark (that's just the opening, not the whole essay - you'd want to write 4-5 paragraphs that size to make sure you nailed the Grade 8 or 9). Can you see how I brought in some of the initial notes I made? I probably wouldn't use them all. They were just there to start me off.

- It doesn't begin with the subject 'you': it gives the reader one concrete image right from the start - the light coming in through the windows. It then brings in the subject: 'You stand…'.

- It uses the cathedral simile, which I quite like and would plan to extend further into the essay.
- It has lyrical, poetic language all the way through: 'streams', 'dust that hangs in the air', 'People like beetles', 'caught black against the sharp sunlight' and so on. All of these are indicating to the examiner that you have a brilliant command of the English language.
- The movement is captured through punctuation: look at how the third sentence is broken up by commas, which makes the reader speed through that sentence mirroring the speed at which people are moving in the station. The repetition of 'moving' helps this as well. Don't be afraid to do things like this. Be brave with your choices. Not many other students will: I can guarantee you that.
- There are reflections from the subject: 'the station having no purpose other than to funnel people to their next destination', 'You don't have time to stop. You never have time.' This is quite powerful mainly because it's so unusual. Not many students will do this either. Yes, it's not description, but remember that this should be subjective so you should have some sort of personality coming through.
- It's using three senses - sight, sound, smell.
- There are specific details: 'Greggs next to platform nine.'
- The final short sentence leaves the reader with something. It is powerful because we have all felt like that at one time or another.

YOUR TURN!

I want you to carry on this piece of writing. Aim for 2 more paragraphs. Use the same style, the same techniques. Try to mirror it as closely as possible. Don't worry if it takes you a while to get it right: revising for this section of the exam is all about practice.

RECAP

- Make sure you **plan**: even if it's just a few minutes to do my note-taking exercise it will get you focusing in on details and thinking originally about how you're going to describe them.
- **Details** are key: try to write in such a way that you're making sure that someone else reading your description can piece together the image in their own mind.
- Be original in the **point of view** you write from. Try third person or even the second person 'you'. Anything that gets the examiner paying a little more attention to your writing.
- Be **poetic**; use the techniques you've learnt when you studied poetry.
- Don't forget the power of **punctuation** to slow down or speed up the reading.

MORE EXAMPLES TO TRY

1. Describe a walk around your local zoo.
2. Describe waking up one morning on a camping trip in the mountains.
3. Describe walking through a busy city like London.
4. Describe your school to an alien who has never seen schools before.
5. Describe a tropical rainforest after a storm.

③

WRITING NARRATIVE(LY)

narrative

/ˈnarətɪv/

noun

noun: **narrative**; plural noun: **narratives**

a spoken or written account of connected events; a story.

This is a useful definition as it tells us straight away the difference between narrative (story) and description. A description is about a moment: you are writing in detail the things you see, hear, smell etc. usually in one location at one point in time. Narrative is all about **connection**: one thing following another from the start of the story to the end.

For those of you who don't read much fiction, and who aren't that interested in writing, narrative is probably the hardest. For that reason, if you get a choice of either narrative or description in your exam, unless you know what you're doing I'd probably go for description.

Why? Because, like description, there are a lot of things that can go wrong and your stories can end up sounding cliched and lacking in interest.

However, a lot of you will have to write creatively for coursework, and if that is the case you'll need to know some rules. If you follow the below you'll be well on your way to writing compelling stories that make your teacher or the examiner really sit up and take notice. As there is nothing better than a well told tale.

For the purposes of this guide I am going to focus on short stories, but the below equally applies to full length novels, as the ingredients of narrative are universal.

THE 6 INGREDIENTS OF GREAT STORIES

I'll go into a lot more detail later, and show these in action as we take an initial idea and turn it into the start of a compelling story, but for now let's think about the most important features of good short stories.

1. They will have an interesting main character supported by a few secondary characters

There are plenty of examples of stories that have only one character, but for the sake of your stories I wouldn't advise it. Short stories need a handful of characters to drive the narrative forward. Without them they can get stuck and be not much more than description or the interior monologue (thoughts) of one character.

It is the **conflict** between characters that moves stories forward. And it is interesting, relatable characters that make readers want to carry on. Anyone who read or watched Game of Thrones will know just how important memorable characters are. When bad things happen to characters we care about it can be pretty shocking.

2. They will have structure

At the most basic level we talk about a beginning, middle and end, but when we go deeper we see it's so much more than that. In a nutshell, a story will begin by setting the scene, before something happens which triggers the main events of the story. These build to a climax, then things calm down again at the end (the main character will have changed in some way through the experience, even if it's just being a bit wiser).

We can summarise it like this:

1. Opening equilibrium (the world is balanced)
2. Inciting incident (disrupts the balance)
3. Chain of events caused by the inciting incident
4. Climax
5. Second, altered equilibrium.

Think about every Hollywood action movie you've seen - they all follow the same structure. Good guy going about his day to day life, some bad guy causes problems, the good guy has to sort the problems out (and gets into more and more danger in the process), bad guy is battled, bad guy loses, good guy goes back to (sort of) normal but is now the hero.

The same with romantic movies. Girl and boy going about their lives, they meet, there are problems, they fall in love sorting out these problems, there is a big challenge but it's ok as they stay together at the end. Or they don't if the ending is bittersweet. Or they die if the ending is tragic (think Romeo and Juliet).

Even the shortest of stories should have some sort of structure. We'll apply that to a real life example later.

3. Their storyline will be driven forward by some sort of conflict (either internal or external)

By conflict I don't necessarily mean anything violent. Conflict can be the inner conflict some characters feel that makes them want to change or it can be two people meeting who are very different and who are forced to spend time with one another (a lot of Christmas family comedy movies use this technique). Whatever the conflict, without it stories lack any sort of energy.

4. They will have specific, concrete settings.

Stories have to be based somewhere. When placing characters in a setting you should follow the same rules as for description. A few details can make all the difference. The opening paragraph at the train station in the last chapter is a good example of how you can begin narrative writing - a man rushing across a station platform, not able to stop to eat even though he's hungry.

5. They will (usually) have dialogue

Dialogue (characters in conversation) is such an important element of stories, yet so many students either overlook it, or are too scared to use it. Yet without it you'll hardly leave the interior of the main character's head, and that can be a lonely (and often quite uninteresting) place to be. There are certain rules for writing dialogue which I'll go into later.

6. They will use suspense to keep the reader interested until the end

This is a tricky one to teach: some writers are better at it than others. However, by withholding certain details from the reader you can create a more suspenseful mood. This is probably the best technique in an exam to get the higher grades, as anything which holds the interest of an exam marker wading through 500 or more exam papers is never going to hurt your chances of a decent grade.

————

Let's take each of these in turn and look at how we might apply them to an exam/coursework situation. We're going to apply the below to November 2018's AQA Paper 2 narrative question:

Write a story about time travel.

HOW TO MAKE UP MEMORABLE CHARACTERS

First off (as I always say): think about what every other student will do and **DO THE OPPOSITE** (that one is worth bold shouty capitals).

What will most students do? Write first person (as themselves). That's their first big mistake. Why? Because it's very hard to generate any interesting point of view if it's you being the narrator. You're better off with a character with a bit of personality from the start.

The first question you ask yourself is: who might be involved in time travel? Jot a few ideas down:

- Scientists
- Evil geniuses
- Mad professor in a university

Ok, I'm going to choose the last one as I think it has the most potential. I'm going to give him a name: Dr Harvey Stone. I can already feel like the story has more potential now I have a crazy professor at the centre.

Now, here's a brilliant tip for you. I only learnt this after years of reading and research into creative writing, but it's actually pretty obvious when you think about it:

Choose a secondary character who is very different from your main character

Think John Watson to Sherlock Holmes, or Banquo to Macbeth: characters who are very much working together, but who are totally different from one another.

Why is this so useful? Because it's their differences that can drive so much interesting dialogue and narrative. Remember: **the more conflict you have in your story, the more interesting it will be**. If everyone was the same and agreed with each other all the time it would make for a very flat story. A bit like life.

Look at it this way: if your mad professor had a long suffering assistant who was very serious and wanted to play it safe all the time, there could be some interesting scenes between them.

Adding more characters

For the amount of time you have to write your story then two main-ish characters will be enough. If you're writing for coursework or just for fun you may bring in more, but as Language exams aren't very long you don't want to go all Game of Thrones and have dozens of walk on parts.

However, if you do plan on more, then they very much will be walk on parts: characters who come into the story briefly. Before including them, you need to ask yourself whether they are necessary to move the storyline on.

This is vital: you should only introduce characters who contribute in some way to the story, or at the very least help you get to know the main character in more detail.

Don't have your Professor going to the shop to buy some biscuits and saying good morning to the shop assistant, or standing chatting to one of his students at the end of the class, **unless by doing so he has a eureka moment and realises how to make his time machine work**. Every detail has to count, as every sentence you write has to count. The examiner will be looking at how you bring the story alive - is your story the one they want to read to the end to see what happens? That, plus decent spelling, punctuation and grammar, are what will get you top marks.

For our time travel Professor, he may land in some other time period and meet someone whose opinion he doesn't agree with. Say a slave owner, or a fascist. It will help us learn about his attitudes to race. That may be an extreme example, but you get my point.

FLESHING OUT THE MAIN CHARACTER: QUICK TIPS

You're obviously not going to have time to create a fully rounded character in the short time you have to write this essay, but you can spend 1-2 minutes brainstorming your main character. Don't worry about what your Professor looks like as you don't need to waste time describing him: instead think about two things: his main strength, and his main personality fault - his weakness, if you like. These are what are driving him to create his time machine and what frame his personality.

His strength is he is a brilliant man, probably the most brilliant in his field. His weakness is that he is angry that no one has recognised how amazing he is. It always seems like his fellow professors are winning all the awards, and he is stuck teaching disinterested students. But he is so close; this is going to be where he shows the world how brilliant he is.

That's it - you don't need any more. You just need his internal motivation, both positive and negative.

Other things you can consider, as they will help you when writing things like dialogue, are how he speaks (slowly, quickly, calmly, aggressively, lots of pauses etc.), and how he moves, his gestures and so on. Imagine you're making a film of your story - what would the audience see that would help them get to know the Professor as quickly as possible?

You don't need to worry about the supporting character as their only function is to help us get to know more about the main character. They have no other purpose. We can see this in action a little later.

HOW TO STRUCTURE YOUR STORY

I would strongly recommend sticking to a very strict structure whether you're writing in an exam or coursework. The tighter the structure, the more familiar it will seem to the examiner, the calmer they will be, and the more likely they are to sprinkle marks like fairy dust onto your exam paper.

Memorise these story elements and jot them down on your exam paper:

1. Establishing scene
2. Inciting event - starts off the storyline properly
3. 2-3 following events
4. Climax
5. Resolution

This is how I would apply these points to my quick essay plan:

1. Professor in lab with assistant - frustrated as knows he's so close. (Establishing scene)
2. Suddenly the time machine works! He cannot believe it. (Inciting event)
3. He gets into it, his assistant warns him of the danger, he ignores him. (Event 1)
4. He dials in 1800, presses the button, arrives in 1800. Meets a slave owner and is appalled by his attitude. (Event 2)
5. Dials in 1600 as he wants to meet Shakespeare, finds him but is disappointed as he's not the hero he thought he'd be. (Event 3)
6. He goes back, dials in 1942, ends up in the blitz with bombs flying overhead. Gets quickly back in. (Event 4 - climax)
7. Back to the present day, tells his assistant that time travel isn't all he thought it would be. (Resolution)

Each of the scenes gets progressively a little more dramatic, towards the final scene where he is almost bombed.

Good idea.... A word on paragraphing

I've a very simple rule when writing narrative. If you change location, time, subject, person speaking or point of view, start a new paragraph. If you do that you can't go far wrong.

ADDING CONFLICT

We can see how the above storyline has plenty of scope for conflict. The professor will be surrounded by people and situations that he will find challenging.

Remember, you don't have to have explosions and car chases in your story (I would strongly advise against trying to describe a car chase with words - give it a go and see what I mean).

What you do need are characters and events that show opposing forces to the main character. So think about how you can challenge the Professor at every point in the story!

This is easier said than done, and you do have to practise. This is where so many students come unstuck: they think they can go into the exam without revising and expect their natural talent to see them through.

I think this is a mistake: although it's not the same sort of revision as for your Literature exam, it's still important to practise these techniques and commit to memory the rules of narrative writing.

The stronger the foundations are, the better your story house will be. You don't want the big bad examiner wolf to blow it down, now do you?

With our time travel story, the conflict is going to come with the 21st Century professor meeting people from other time periods. He will be disappointed, shocked and terrified by what he sees.

You don't need to plan much of this out as you've already decided on his character and roughly where he's going to go. That's enough.

DECIDING ON SETTING(S)

For an exam, no more than 1-2 settings, possibly only one. I've chosen four above, but to be honest it may be too many. I might only get to write the first two locations, or I may only write a short paragraph or two about one of them.

What you don't want to do is have your main character going on some huge journey to a hundred different places meeting lots of people. Keep it simple.

When describing setting, this is where your descriptive writing revision will come in handy. Remind yourself of the points I made in the last chapter. Focus in on a few small details. Use more than one sense. Bring in some poetic language if you can. All of these will build both place and mood.

Do you want to communicate how stressed your character is feeling? Maybe reflect it in the weather. Perhaps you want to show how frustrated he or she is?

Think about how the environment can almost get in the way, such as a stuck kitchen drawer or wading through mud when they're in a hurry.

In the same way that you want the characters' actions and speech to add to the story, you want the setting to do the same.

For our time travel story, we will start in the Professor's lab in the university. We'll think about what sort of equipment he has around him, maybe describe the time machine but not necessarily say what it is at first. This will immediately build suspense.

When we change location we may focus on how different it seems to the Professor, or perhaps how similar. This can be used to either emphasise how much the world has changed, or how some things remain the same.

Again, it's the small details that will count, and focusing on more than only one sense. England at the time of Shakespeare would have been quite a smelly place, for example.

WRITING DIALOGUE

I won't lie: students are usually rubbish at writing dialogue. Actually, not only students. Anyone who isn't an experienced writer tends to fall flat on their face when they try to effectively capture how people speak.

The golden rule is: don't try to mirror normal speech patterns as you'll end up making your characters sound vague, weak and annoying. Take this as an example:

'Hello, er, welcome to my, um, presentation, where I, I, I'll be going through the latest, er, features of our exciting new product. It is, um, an honour to be here.'

Now, if you heard that spoken, you'd not think much about it. When we listen to people we actually tune out a lot of the ums and ers (unless they dominate, in which case we end up focusing on them).

But with writing all we see are these pointless extra words that add nothing. It's the same with repetition: we actually repeat ourselves quite a lot, but there's no need to do it when we write dialogue.

The only exception to this is when you're deliberately wanting your character to sound vague, weak or annoying, and even then it should be used sparingly...

How to structure dialogue

It's important to set out dialogue in the correct way on the page. There are no exceptions to this so don't try to experiment.

- **New speaker = new line**. Whenever there is change of speaker, you start a new line and indent like a new paragraph:

'Hi James,' Sarah said.

'Hi Sarah,' James replied.

'How are you?' asked Sarah.

'I'm very well. You?' James replied.

- **Look at how the above is punctuated.** If you are

going to add a speech tag (he said, she said) then you should generally use a comma after the speech but before the closed speech mark. However, if you aren't going to use a tag, then use a full stop. The exception is if you use a question mark or exclamation mark:

'How are you?' David asked.

Sarah looked at him and smiled. 'I'm very well.'

'That's great!' David shook her hand.

- **Don't always add speech tags.** It's better to sometimes add a tag (he said, she said etc.), and sometimes get characters speaking whilst doing things.

David walked up to the group standing by the buffet. 'What's good for breakfast this morning?'

The man nearest the bacon shrugged. 'Don't know, we haven't eaten yet either.'

David smiled. 'Good point,' he said.

- **Don't try to add every tiny unimportant thing to the dialogue.** Only use it if it moves the action of the story along. Compare the first example below to the second:

Example 1

'Hi,' Jeff said.

'Hello,' Jill replied.

'How's your day been so far?' Jeff asked.

'Not too bad. Nice weather,' Jill answered.

'Yes, it is. I don't know about you, but a lot of these creative writing exam papers are so bad, aren't they?'

Jill nodded. 'Yes, they are. Really awful. It's a good job some of them read the Examiner's Head essay writing guide.'

Jeff smiled. 'Yes, that's very true. Thank goodness!'

Example 2

Jeff sighed and looked up from the exam papers. 'Wow,' he said. 'Some of these are so bad.'

Jill nodded. 'Good job some of them read the Examiner's Head book.'

Jeff smiled. 'Ha! Very true.'

All we really care about in this short scene is what the two exam markers (maybe a husband and wife team? Who knows) think about the papers they've been marking. The rest adds nothing. Make sure you only write dialogue if it either tells you something about the character or moves things along. Ideally both. So get rid of the hi and how are you and nice day stuff. No one cares, least of all the exam marker.

ADDING SUSPENSE

As I say above, it's quite hard to teach this, but I can give you a few tips that work. Your ultimate goal is to keep the reader hooked until the end. This is why the Roald Dahl twist in the tale stories are so popular. If you've not read any, I'd thoroughly recommend them as part of your story writing revision. *Lamb to the Slaughter* is one of my personal favourites.

Try adding one or two of these and see how it spices up your story:

- Hint at what is to come: this is most effective when you're writing the story as if you're looking back on events. For our Professor, you might start the story like this: 'If Professor Harvey Stone had known what to expect when he first decided to build a time machine, he might have had second thoughts.' This is a brilliant way to immediately get the reader wondering why he'd think like that.

- Have a character suggest that a particular course of action is a bad idea. The reader will want to know if they were right:

'But Professor, I think building a time machine and going back to the time of the second world war is a really bad idea,' Sarah said.

'Don't worry, Sarah. What could possibly go wrong?' replied the Professor.

- When writing a suspenseful scene, use particular trigger words that build atmosphere. Certain adjectives can help: 'slowly, carefully, the Professor stepped from the time machine... He suddenly stopped, unable to believe what he was seeing.'
- Which brings me to my next point. You know in horror movies when you see the terrified reaction of a character before you see what they're looking at? You're left thinking 'what, what are you looking at that's so terrifying?' and your mind fills with what it could be. You can do the same with writing. I've just suggested it above. If you write something like 'the Professor stared in amazement. He had never seen anything like it before' then your readers will want to know what he's looking at! It's a simple but effective technique.
- You can also use dialogue to build suspense and tension. If one of the characters are really unsure, as a reader we tend to identify with them:

'Professor, I'm just not sure about this. Are you sure it's ok?' Sarah asked, gripping the controller with both hands.

The Professor laughed, but a bead of sweat ran down his face...

Good idea...Show don't tell

Classic beginner error this one, so worth a quick aside to explore. So many students fall into the trap of telling the reader how a character is feeling rather than showing them. An example would be saying 'Sarah was scared' rather than 'Sarah's heart beat faster and her palms became sweaty.' Wherever possible, try to **show** the reader how a character **physically** reacts to things. It's so much more interesting than telling us all the time.

APPLYING ALL THE ABOVE TO OUR STORY

We've played around with a few ideas, but now it's time to show them in action. I won't write the whole story, but as with the descriptive writing I'll ask you to carry the story on in the exact same style and consciously using all the techniques I've explained above.

If your revision involves writing lots of short stories then who knows? Maybe you'll get a taste for it and I'll see your name in print one day. Writing is one of the most amazing things to do, so I hope that's the case for some of you!

The Time Machine

The room fell silent. The Professor looked to his assistant and nodded. Sarah, as always unsure of her boss's ideas and even less sure about what she was about to do, gulped. The moment of truth. Would it work?

It had been years in the planning. The Professor had given up so much to make it happen. Missed the awards, saw his colleagues earn huge salaries when they sold out to big business. But not him. Not Harvey Stone. And now it would all be worth it. He could sense how close he was.

'Ok Sarah, let's see if she finally works.'

Sarah frowned. 'But are you sure, Professor? I mean, we tried it last week with a mouse and look what happened.'

The Professor brushed off her concern with a wave of the hand. 'Teething trouble, nothing more,' he said. 'You worry too much.'

'Perhaps, but only because you never seem to worry yourself.'

'Life is too short,' the Professor said.

He looked at the machine. It was a thing of beauty. A little taller than a human, it was shaped like a giant bell, its white surface covered with dials and flashing lights. He had to admit that some of the lights were only there for show, and he liked the low humming noise they gave off. He needed it to look, and sound, right. He wanted to prove to the world that he could create something no one had created before.

It was his time machine, and today he was going on a journey into the unknown.

As I hope you can see, I've tried to use a few techniques. I brought in the contrast between the characters, added some suspenseful dialogue, and described the time machine using sight and sound. We get the impression of a passionate, driven man, but also one who is a bit vain (the lights for show give that away). It could be interesting to see his arrogance challenged when he meets people from the past…

NOW IT'S YOUR TURN

I want you to carry on this story to the end, using the structure I suggested earlier. If you like you can change the places he goes, but ultimately you want him to be disappointed and realise that the present day is probably the best place for him to be.

A FEW MORE IDEAS FOR YOU TO PRACTISE

Try to practise these in the time available for the exam. If it's an hour, spend 10-15 minutes planning, 40-45 minutes writing and try to give yourself 5 minutes at the end to read through. I know we teachers say that all the time and you students never do, but it might make a whole grade's difference if you spot something glaringly obvious (such as forgetting to paragraph then inserting the universal // symbol where the paragraphs should be).

- Write about a holiday that goes very badly wrong.
- Write about a child's first trick or treat experience.
- Write about someone's first halloween… as a ghost.
- Write about someone who can see into the future.
- Write about someone finding an abandoned puppy.
- Write about someone who suddenly finds they have a superpower.

4

WRITING ANALYTICALLY

analysis

/əˈnalɪsɪs/

noun

noun: **analysis**; plural noun: **analyses**

detailed examination of the elements or structure of something.

Analysis is what sorts the men from the boys (or the women from the girls), the wheat from the chaff, the haves from the have nots. It's the ultimate test of your English genius, and it's the one students struggle with the most.

In essence, **an analytical essay takes evidence from a text and explains how it answers a question.** Analysis is about exploring ideas on a text.

The key word in the definition above is **detailed**: good analysis will **say a lot about a little, rather than a little about a lot.**

It will dig deep into a text, pull out lots of relevant small details, and say interesting things about them. More on that later.

The other useful part of the definition is that it refers to both 'elements' and 'structure'. This is important in English Language and Literature analysis.

You're going to be writing both about the **words themselves** and **how they are structured** (i.e. laid out on the page).

This isn't only for poetry - non-fiction, novels and plays also use structural techniques to guide how something is read or performed.

BUT WHERE DO I START?

Planning for an analytical essay isn't easy. I know that. You need to first of all understand exactly what the questions is asking you to do, before find the relevant quotes in the text and exploring how they answer the question.

This does take practice: my suggestion to you is start with small paragraphs on passages and work up to whole essays.

You need first of all to learn how to structure an analytical sentence, before working on linking them together into a paragraph before linking paragraphs into an essay.

The best analogy I can use is digging for buried treasure. You start near the surface, perhaps unearthing one or two gold coins as you do so.

With every sentence and every paragraph so you dig deeper into the text, saving your most profound analysis (the real treasure) for the end. You'll see what I mean later.

I'll start by going through the ingredients of analytical writing. I'll then refer you to a section from one of the other books in the Examiner's Head series, Macbeth GCSE English Literature Revision Guide. In that book I go through the play in lots of detail before showing you how to answer exam questions.

I'll then show you how you can apply these ideas to tackling the analysis questions in the English Language exam, referring to my section on writing analysis from another book in the Examiner's Head series: AQA GCSE English Language 9-1 Revision Guide.

(Do check it out as it has lots of useful stuff on how you tackle every question in that exam.)

THE INGREDIENTS OF ANALYTICAL WRITING

Although I know that lots of you worry about writing analysis, you really shouldn't. If you follow the below you should find it fairly straightforward.

1. You should always begin by understanding exactly what the question is asking you to do

This may seem a bit 'duh obvious' but you'd be surprised at how many exam essays I've marked where the student has totally missed the point of the question. Let's look at a few examples of the sort of questions you might get so we can see what each one is asking.

The first question is from an English Language exam. It will give you two passages, a few paragraphs long, and ask you to **compare and contrast**. We'll look at how to tackle this sort of question later:

1. Compare the ways these two texts present the life of a writer.

You should consider:

how they use language and structure

the ideas in the texts

The next question asks you to focus on **structure:**

2. How has the writer structured the text to interest you as a reader? You could write about:

what the writer focuses your attention on at the beginning

how and why this focus <u>develops and changes</u> as the text continues

any other <u>structural features</u> that interest you.

Finally, it's about how the writer uses **language**:

3. How does the writer use <u>language</u> here to describe ...?

You could include the writer's choice of:

words and phrases

language features and techniques

sentence forms

These are the main three you'll get in a Language exam. The most important thing here is that you spend a minute or so underlining the key words in the question, exactly as I've done above.

This will keep you on track and stop you from only writing about language when you should be writing about structure, for example.

In a **Literature** exam, you'll likely get a question on either character, setting or theme. Here are some examples. Again, look at the words I've underlined:

Question 1: Macbeth

Starting with this extract, how does Shakespeare present Macbeth as a <u>powerful</u> character?

Write about:

- how Shakespeare presents Macbeth as a powerful character <u>in this extract</u>

- how Shakespeare presents Macbeth as a powerful character <u>in the play as a whole</u>

Question 2: An Inspector Calls

How and why does Sheila change in An Inspector Calls? Write about:

- how Sheila responds to her family and to the Inspector

- how Priestley presents Sheila by the ways he writes.

Question 3: Poetry anthology

Compare how poets present attitudes towards a parent in 'Follower' and in one other poem from 'Love and relationships'.

2. You should then find the quotes that answer the question

Take your pen or pencil and simply underline where in the passage/novel/play/poem you see examples that will support your answer - but only if these are quotes you plan to use in your answer. Aim to underline no more than 4-5 word quotes where possible - sometimes individual words are best.

What you want to avoid is writing out great long quotes in your exam as it won't allow you to dig deeply into them and the examiner is able to read the text as well. Far better to choose 2 or 3 words in a passage and insert them into your analysis. I'll show you how to do that later.

3. Use a specific technique for inserting quotes into your answer

I see so many students get this wrong: what is most important is that **the quotes should feed into the sentence: the sentence should make grammatical sense with the quotes inserted.**

Let me show you an example from a Language exam. Let's say you have a passage like this and are asked to explain how the writer uses language to describe Dorrigo's fear:

Hands wet with sweat on the wheel, panting heavily, Dorrigo Evans weighed their options. They were all bad. The road out in either direction was now completely cut off – by the burning tree in front of them and the fire front behind them. He wiped his hands in turn on his shirt and trousers. They were trapped. He turned to his children in the back seat. He felt sick. They were holding each other, eyes white and large in their sooty faces.

The wrong way to do it would be like this:

'Dorrigo Evans showed he was scared "Hands wet with sweat". He was very nervous "wiped his hands" and so were his children "eyes white and large"'.

The correct way would be like this:

'Dorrigo Evans shows his fear through having "Hands wet with sweat" and the fact he is "panting heavily". We know his family are also scared because their eyes are "white and large in their sooty faces"'.

See the difference? If you remove the speech marks from the first answer it makes no sense. The second one reads fine with or without the speech marks.

Top tip…. If you struggle to feed your quote into a sentence you can put it in brackets, like this: 'It is clear that Dorrigo is nervous ("Hands wet with sweat on the wheel") because his options "were all bad"'. Don't use that too often but it can be helpful if you can't work out how to make the sentence flow with the quote inserted.

4. Write analysis in the present tense - otherwise it can sound like a history essay

Look at the two examples above. The poorly written one is in the past tense, the well written one in the present tense. The second example is better as analysis flows better if you write in the present tense. This is because you're writing about a passage you're reading in the present moment, not in the past.

5. Use linking words and phrases to seamlessly direct the reader through your answer

This can make all the difference and can enable you to write a lot more in a short space of time and not repeat yourself too much. There are words and phrases to show you're analysing, continuing on an idea, contrasting ideas, and summing up.

Here are some of most useful examples:

Analysing:

'This suggests…'

'This shows us that…'

'This demonstrates…'

'The writer is insinuating that…'

'The writer is suggesting that…'

'The writer seems to suggest that…'

'This demonstrates….'

'This gives us the impression that…'

Continuing an idea:

'This is developed by…'

'The writer further develops this by….'

'We see this developed when…'

'The writer further explores this by…'

'Furthermore,…'

'Moreover,…'

'In addition,…'

Contrasting ideas:

'However,…'

'In contrast…'

'Contrastingly…'

'Conversely…'

'In comparison…'

'Whilst the first writer suggests… the second suggests…'

Concluding:

'In conclusion,…'

'In summary,…'

———

We'll see some of these in action later.

USING ASSESSMENT OBJECTIVES

I know that many of you find any mention of Assessment Objectives (or AOs as they're affectionately abbreviated) either terrifying or incredibly tedious. They need be neither. All they are is a tick-list against which you write your answer. By ticking off each you're guaranteed a good mark.

The reason for that is that the whole point of AOs is to give exam markers a guide for what to look for when they're marking. It's helpful before we look at sample questions and answers to see what these are.

The below is taken from AQA's English Literature mark scheme, but they could apply to any Literature exam as all the exam boards work to the same set of criteria agreed by the UK's Department for Education. So no matter your exam board (Edexcel, WJEC or whatever), a Grade 5 will be a Grade 5 and a Grade 9 will look and feel broadly the same.

A low grade (3-4)

- Students who get around a Grade 4 will write **a few generally relevant comments** on the text but will tend to lapse in retelling the story (AO1).
- They will **identify some of the methods** the writer uses but are unlikely to say much about the effect they have (AO2).
- They have **some awareness of context** but find it hard to link this to the text (AO3).
- They are **inconsistent with their spelling etc** and write with simple sentences without much variety (AO4).

A mid grade (5-6)

Students who get around a Grade 5-6 will write a **clear response with suitable references** (AO1). They will make **clear references to the writer's methods** to support their points (AO2). **Clear links** will made with some aspects of historical context (AO3). Spelling and punctuation is **generally pretty good** and there's a **wider range** of sentences and vocabulary (AO4).

A good grade (7-8)

This will show **very effective understanding** and careful use of references and quotes (AO1). It will **analyse carefully and comment consistently well**, **interpreting** ideas (AO2). **Very effective links** will be made between context and text (AO3). Spelling etc. will be **generally excellent** (AO4).

A very good grade (8-9)

- This will show a **broad, conceptualised idea** of the text, backed up by **well-judged and wide-ranging references and quotations** (AO1).
- It will **analyse and explore** texts precisely and convincingly. There will be **finely tuned comment** on language, form and structure (AO2).
- A **wide range of contextual factors** will be convincingly and relevantly written about (AO3).

- Spelling etc will be **very accurate** and meaning will be **clearly controlled** (AO4).

As you can see, there are certain key words that stand out depending on the level you're writing at:

- **Low** answers will be basic, making some relevant responses and referring to some writing features. However, these answers tend towards retelling chunks of the text rather than analysing. (If you're not sure what I mean by analysing don't worry: I'll come on to that.)
- **Mid** answers will be clearer in both their response and reference to methods, and will generally be well written.
- **Good** answers will show analysis - understanding themes and ideas exploring the effect of writer's methods.
- **Very good** answers will be controlled, detailed, intelligent, insightful and very well written. They will go deeply into the text and show originality and flair.

Don't worry if you don't think you can achieve the very highest grades: if you stick to my rules you'll give yourself a far better chance of getting up into the 6s and 7s as a minimum.

Language AOs are similar. A low grade will make basic references to the text and not say much, a mid grade will make suitable references to the text and will make some interesting points, and a high grade will use lots of detail from the text and say some original things.

Very high grades (8 and 9) go that bit further every time, coming up with a lot of original ideas and writing with intelligence and confidence.

5

ANSWERING A LANGUAGE ANALYSIS QUESTION

Let's start by looking at how we'd answer an analysis question in a Language exam. These exams tend to give you 4 questions on a text. The first two questions are quite straightforward, asking you to take detail direct from the text. The third and fourth tend to focus on analysis.

THE QUESTION

Let's start by looking at AQA's Paper 2 Language (non fiction) question, taken from November 2018. You can find all these papers published freely on the AQA website. I'll start with Question 3 which you can find here. If you're reading the print version of this guide, go to aqa.org.uk and search for English Language GCSE.

3. You now need to refer only to **Source B** from **lines 8 to 18**.

How does the writer use language to describe her first experiences of cycling?

[12 marks]

Here is the section of the non fiction text you have to refer to. It is taken from a 19th Century newspaper article on cycling. You can find the full insert here:

Riding on a track began to bore me as soon as I had learnt to balance, but I remained steadily practising until I could turn easily, cut figures of eight, get on and off quickly on either side and stop without charging into unwelcome obstacles. This done, burning to try my fate in traffic, and yet as nervous as a hare that feels the greyhound's breath, I launched my little bicycle early one Sunday morning in July into the stormy oceans of Sloane Street, on my way to visit a sick friend who lived about four miles off. The streets were really very clear, but I shall never forget my terror. I arrived in about two hours, streaming and exhausted, much more in need of assistance than the invalid I went to visit. Coming home it was just as bad; I reached my house about three o'clock and went straight to bed, where I had my lunch, in a state bordering on collapse. I only recount this adventure in order to encourage others who may have had the same experience as myself, but who may not have tried to conquer their nervousness.

PLANNING THE ANSWER

Remember what I said above? Of course you do as I know you're hanging on my every word (ok, maybe not). Quickly underline the key words in the question. Can you see what they are? This one is quite easy. 'Language' and 'first experiences of cycling'. So you don't have to refer to anything structural, such as sentence length, order of events or paragraphing.

Then, underline the key words and phrases in the passage that tell you about how she feels about cycling for the first time. You'll likely do something like this:

Riding on a track <u>began to bore</u> me as soon as I had learnt to balance, but I remained steadily practising until I could turn <u>easily</u>, <u>cut figures of eight</u>, get on and off <u>quickly</u> on either side and stop without charging into unwelcome obstacles. This done, burning to try my fate in traffic, and yet as nervous as a hare that feels the greyhound's breath, I launched my little bicycle early one Sunday morning in July into the stormy oceans of Sloane Street, on my way to visit a sick friend who lived about four miles off. The streets were really very clear, but I shall never forget my terror. I arrived in about two hours, streaming and exhausted, much more in need of assistance than the invalid I went to visit. Coming home it was just as bad; I reached my house about three o'clock and went straight to bed, where I had my lunch, in a state bordering on collapse. I only recount this adventure in order to encourage others who may have had the same experience as myself, but who may not have tried to conquer their nervousness.

Plenty to work with here! I would then suggest going through the passage in order, beginning with what she first says, going on to show how that develops and ending with how she feels once she's ended her journey. In general, it's much easier to analyse in order rather than jumping around. The same can be said about analysing characters in a literature text. Even poems tend to be easier to write about when you show how the poet develops their ideas on a subject through their poem.

YOUR TURN!

Have a go at the above, aiming to spend no more than 15 minutes actually writing (as the question is worth 12 marks and I tend to suggest spending around one minute per mark). Use the linking words and phrases I suggest above if they help. Then, compare with my version below and see how yours differs.

MY VERSION

The writer begins by explaining that riding on a track 'began to bore her', which suggests she feels that riding a bicycle is a simple thing to do. This is further emphasised by how she could 'turn easily' and 'cut figures of eight', the latter sounding almost balletic, as if she is so accomplished on the bicycle that she can do far more than only ride in a straight line. She is clearly impatient to try out her skills on the road, saying that she is 'burning to try [her] fate in traffic'. The word 'fate' is interesting as it foreshadows what is to follow: it prepares the reader for the drama of her actually cycling on the road.

The extended nautical metaphor ('I launched my little bicycle.....into the stormy seas') is effective because, like a stormy sea, the road and its traffic is unknown to the writer. It also suggests her nervousness in venturing out into danger. What follows are several emotive words which capture well the emotions the writer experienced that day: 'terror.....streaming and exhausted...bordering on collapse'. She is clearly traumatised by the experience and captures it well.

Hopefully you can see the techniques I've used here:

- going chronologically (in time order) through the passage;
- feeding quotes into each sentence so they make sense;
- using linking words and phrases to both show analysis is happening and to move the reader through the analysis;
- using brackets to drop a quote into a sentence;
- digging deeply into certain words and phrases.

DIGGING DEEP

I learnt a good tip at university: I wish I'd known it earlier. I mentioned it at the start of this chapter:

Say a lot about a little, rather than a little about a lot.

What this means is simple. Don't feel you have to write about every single sentence in a passage. You don't. If you try to do that all you'll end up doing is summarising the passage which will get you a grade 4, 5 at best.

What you should instead do is focus in on a few words, say one thing about them, then say another thing. Say a third thing if you can! You can see examples of this above:

> She is clearly <u>impatient</u> to try out her skills on the road, saying that she is 'burning to try [her] fate in traffic'. The word 'fate' is interesting as it <u>foreshadows</u> what is to follow: it <u>prepares the reader</u> for the drama of her actually cycling on the road.

One quote, three ideas: introduced by explaining her impatience, bringing in foreshadowing, and explaining the effect of this on the reader. It's this sort of depth of analysis you need to show to achieve grades 8 and 9. The colon (:) is a brilliant bit of punctuation, as what is basically says to the examiner is 'look out, some clever and thoughtful analysis is coming!'

CLEVER BRACKETS

Notice also I do something unusual with square brackets. This is a pretty advanced technique, but I see no reason for you not to use it. I used it to substitute 'her' for 'my'. Why? Because I want the whole sentence to be about *my* analysis of *her*, and if I leave in 'my' it reads a little awkwardly. Will you lose marks if you don't use square brackets? No, not at all. But you'll impress the examiner if you do!

⑥

ANSWERING A LITERATURE ANALYSIS QUESTION

There is very little difference with how you approach Literature analysis. You're going to work out what the question is asking, find short quotes and words to back up your ideas, use linking words and phrases, and go deep into the text wherever possible.

The main addition with Literature is that you're going to be writing about a whole novel, play or group of poems, and you'll make reference to social and historical context.

I won't go into lots of detail about that here: you can check out what I mean by taking a look at my Literature revision guides.

Let's have a look at an AQA GCSE Literature question and some sample answers. This is taken from my Macbeth revision guide. Do check it out if you're doing Macbeth as I go through the play in depth as well as show you how to answer different sorts of questions.

As I mention before, the exam board this refers to is irrelevant: every exam is testing you on the same skills. You can find the Macbeth guide here, or search for Examiner's Head Macbeth in Amazon.

SECTION A: SHAKESPEARE

Answer **one** question from this section on your chosen text.

Read the following extract from Act 1 Scene 5 of *Macbeth* and then answer the question that follows.

At this point in the play Lady Macbeth is speaking. She has just received the news that King Duncan will be spending the night at her castle.

The raven himself is hoarse

That croaks the fatal entrance of Duncan

Under my battlements. Come, you spirits

That tend on mortal thoughts, unsex me here,

And fill me from the crown to the toe topfull

Of direst cruelty; make thick my blood,

Stop up th'access and passage to remorse

That no compunctious visitings of nature

Shake my fell purpose nor keep peace between

Th'effect and it. Come to my woman's breasts,

And take my milk for gall, you murd'ring ministers,

Wherever in your sightless substances

You wait on nature's mischief. Come, thick night,

And pall thee in the dunnest smoke of hell,

That my keen knife see not the wound it makes

Nor heaven peep through the blanket of the dark,

To cry 'Hold, hold!'

Starting with this speech, explain how far you think Shakespeare presents Lady Macbeth as a powerful woman.

Write about:

how Shakespeare presents Lady Macbeth in this speech

how Shakespeare presents Lady Macbeth in the play as a whole.

[30 marks]

AO4 [4 marks]

HOW TO TACKLE THIS QUESTION

Here's a foolproof way of tackling this in the exam. You can use this approach for any character-based question. You'll notice some repetition with the Language approach above, and that's for a reason. The approach is very similar.

1. First of all, make sure you understand exactly what the **question** is asking of you. I'd always suggest **underlining the key words**, and making sure that every single thing you write in response refers in some way to those words. In this case it is about how far you think Lady Macbeth is presented as a powerful woman. Not just that she is presented as a powerful woman, but *how far*. So you can say how she may not be so powerful, which makes sense as the play progresses. These small details are important!

2. Now, you'll focus in on the **exam paper passage**. Underline anything which refers to Lady Macbeth being powerful. Nothing else: just any words and phrases which suggest power to us.

3. Next, you'll go through **the entire play** and find other examples which show her being powerful. Underline them and make a note of the page reference *on your answer paper*. Don't worry too much at this point about Act, Scene and Line numbers - just jot down the page reference and a brief note as to how it answers the question. The reason you

want to put all your planning on your answer paper is that if you run out of time the examiner may still give you marks if you make relevant notes. Remember to look at the formal elements as well - if it's written in blank verse, particular uses of punctuation maybe or line breaks. Anything which adds to your understanding of how Lady Macbeth seems powerful.

4. I'd then suggest you jot down a **quick paragraph plan** so you know the order in which you'll write. Chronologically (order of events) is perfectly fine with character studies - in fact I'd usually suggest this as it makes it easier to show how a character might change (which is very much the case with Lady Macbeth as she loses power as the play progresses). It might look something like this:

5. First impressions - first things she says, how she appears to Macbeth

6. How she convinces Macbeth to do the deed. Her reaction to Macbeth when he murders the king

7. Macbeth's response to her when she asks him about Banquo

8. How she acts during the banqueting scene and how this shows her losing power

9. How she ends the play and why (loss of power, madness)

10. Summary of points and whether you think she is powerful or not

11. 4-5 paragraphs is enough for an exam essay like this. Writing this short plan will help keep you focused, as everything you write in that paragraph will link to the subject of the paragraph and the key words in the question. Notice I don't include an introduction? In an exam, with a limited amount of time, I would always suggest getting straight into the analysis. Introductions can often look like the candidate is writing their way into the exam. But because you've done a paragraph plan there'll be no chance of that happening with you, will there.

12. Begin every paragraph with a **short, punchy sentence** which shows the examiner exactly what you're going to be

writing about in that paragraph and helps keep you on track:

13. 'In the passage, Lady Macbeth is presented as a woman with immense power.'

14. 'When we are first introduced to Lady Macbeth we are presented with a woman concerned that her husband won't have the strength to become king.'

15. 'Lady Macbeth shows her strength and power both before and after Duncan's murder.'

16. For those of you who've read my English Language book (do give it a go - I think it's quite useful), you'll know I have a certain way of structuring analysis. You'll probably have heard of PEE - Point, Evidence, Explanation - and that's ok. However, I prefer **PEAL - Point, Evidence, Analysis, Link**. Why? Because it's important that you show how your ideas develop throughout the paragraph. An examiner will be looking at this carefully. If you offer one quote and say one thing about it, you're looking at a Grade 4 or 5. If you say 2-3 things, adding detail and **making links between quotes**, you'll be moving up to the Grade 7, 8, or more.

17. Remember that you are writing a Literature essay, not a Language essay. And as such you have to make sure you include something on **context**. In this case you'd be referring to the typical role and representation of women and how Lady Macbeth goes against this (and what happens to her as a result). Don't forget that AO3 context is worth 6 marks.

18. The other key thing to make sure you do is write about the techniques Shakespeare uses. You need to make sure you use the right terminology: metaphor/figurative language, simile and so on. This is part of AO2 and is worth 12 marks.

EXEMPLAR PARAGRAPHS AND THE GRADES THEY'D GET

It's time to look at a few examples. I won't write entire essays below, but rather share with you a few paragraphs and ask you to suggest what sort of grade they might get. You can refer back to the last section and imagine you are the examiner. What evidence do you see that would get the student a particular grade?

Remember - these aren't whole essays - just sample paragraphs.

Example 1

Lady Macbeth is a powerful woman in the play. In this section she is talking about not wanting to be a woman anymore and being filled with cruelty. When she says 'come you spirits' she means that she wants evil spirits to come to her. This is because she needs some help from them. This is before they murder Duncan. After this she talks about her woman's breasts and murdering ministers. She ends the speech by wanting night to come so no one can see what they do. She wants to be unsexed because at the time women had no rights so she doesn't think being a woman will allow her to kill the king.

Example 2

In this passage from the play, Lady Macbeth is summoning evil spirits to give her power. She begins by saying 'come you spirits', as if she is casting a spell to call them to her. She wants them to remove her femininity - she says 'unsex me here' which means she wants them to stop her from feeling anything so she and Macbeth can murder the king. This is because she thinks that being a woman will make her weaker. This was a common way of thinking at the time the play was written as people didn't see women as being powerful. The phrase 'make thick my blood' is an interesting one as it suggests her blood needs to be made thicker in order to gain more power to commit the murder. The sounds of the words also add to that feeling as the words themselves sound thick. When she says 'stop up the access and passage to remorse' she wants the spirits to make sure she no longer feels any guilt for killing Duncan.

Example 3

Whilst the play is set in the 11th Century, Lady Macbeth is very much a product of the era in which Shakespeare was writing. She knows that, if she wishes to have the power to go through with the 'deed' she will need to have her femininity removed. This soliloquy, which comes just before the arrival of Macbeth back to the castle, is a potent reminder of how weak women were seen in general, and therefore how much they relied on the supernatural in order to gain the power they did not inherently possess. She begins by summoning up the 'spirits who tend on mortal thoughts' and demands 'unsex me here': in order to summon up this power she needs to have her femininity removed. It is not a request, it is a demand: she is not acting in any way as one would expect a woman of the time to act. Language like 'direst cruelty' and 'make thick my blood' are deeply sinister, the sounds of the words themselves adding to this effect: the consonance of 'make thick' is particularly effective. She equates 'remorse' with being female: she wants this to be stopped up as she sees this as a part of female 'nature' that she has to have removed. It is only in this way that she will gain the power she so desperately craves.

Three responses, three very different grades. Have you worked them out?

If I was an examiner, I would give the first around a Grade 4, the second around a Grade 6, and if Student 3 carried on like that they'd be on their way to a Grade 9 no question.

Helpful?

Let's dig into them in a bit more detail and see where marks were picked up, and indeed dropped...

Example 1

…is clearly written, doesn't use any complex language, and does show some understanding: the second sentence shows that.

There is evidence of using quotations and a basic understanding of what the quotation means. However, the second half of the paragraph lapses into retelling the plot, with no explanation.

There is a little evidence of context but it feels like the candidate has stuck this at the end because they remembered they had to. It is also not very well linked back into the play: women's rights and killing kings don't necessarily go together. There are a couple of spelling mistakes in there as well.

Example 2

…is a little better: it shows a more detailed understanding of the play, uses quotes more effectively, and begins to analyse: phrases such as 'as if' and 'this is because' are examples of what I call 'analytical signposts' - indicators to the examiner that you are about to explain the quote in some depth (more on that below).

The candidate mentions some language techniques but there is no technical language used. There is some relevant contextual detail but it's a little superficial ('a common way of thinking at the time': Which time? What way of thinking?)

Example 3

…is as good as you'd get at GCSE - in fact if I read this I'd think this person was ready for A-Level. I don't say this to put you off, but rather to give you the ingredients so you can give the top grade your best shot. I like the way the paragraph begins with context that frames everything that follows.

It is specific - the candidate places the representation of women both within the historical period of the play but also the time in which it was written.

There is technical language in there (soliloquy, consonance), and the analysis is excellent - every time the candidate says one thing, they say something more - the reference to the demand, specific detail about language techniques.

They show real control of how to use quotation, taking individual words and weaving them into their sentences. The paragraph ends with a simple yet insightful closing comment. Language is sophisticated throughout: inherently, summoning, craves.

Why don't we now look at how to craft the Grade 8-9 paragraph in even more depth? I thought that would make you happy.

7

AIMING FOR THE TOP GRADES WITH ANALYTICAL WRITING

Drum roll: the moment you've been waiting for. Below I give you a few tips for how to write killer paragraphs. I refer to this in a previous section but it's worth really picking out the most useful ingredients of top essays.

If you use these tips, do lots of practice essays, and make sure you know the play text back to front (which if you have read my Macbeth Revision Guide and made notes in your play you will have done), I can pretty well guarantee you an improved grade.

What I can't (sadly) do is guarantee you a Grade 9: it is safe to say that some candidates just have more natural ability and are able to say more original things than others. However, if you follow these ingredients you will have a far firmer foundation on which to excel, and are therefore more likely to achieve these top grades. So, give yourself every chance and follow these steps.

Here are the top 5 things to remember!

1. SAY A LOT ABOUT A LITTLE, RATHER THAN A LITTLE ABOUT A LOT.

I've mentioned this twice before, and there's a reason. It is so important! It's the single biggest differentiator between ok essays and brilliant essays. **It is far better to take a few small details and say as much as you can about them, rather than try to write about an entire passage or quote a long piece of text.** In fact, I would go as far as to say that Grades 8&9 essays tend to quote no more than 4-5 words at any one time, as this forces you to go deep.

As an example, take the final section of the passage:

Come, thick night,

And pall thee in the dunnest smoke of hell,

That my keen knife see not the wound it makes

Nor heaven peep through the blanket of the dark,

To cry 'Hold, hold!'

Now, a Grade 5 or 6 candidate might quote the whole thing, which is rather a waste of time as the examiner also has the passage in front of them (bet you didn't know that… oh, you did).

It's much better to pick out key words and feed them into your analysis, and say as much as you possibly can about them.

Think about all three AOs when you're writing as if you can say three things about a short quote you're on a winner!

You obviously won't do this for every single quote, but it's worth seeing if you can extend your ideas just that bit further each time:

Lady Macbeth ends her soliloquy by asking the 'thick night' to cover her so that her 'keen knife see not the wound it makes'. 'Thick' in this context refers to the night being unfeeling: by personifying night she seems to suggest that the night becomes an accomplice in her crime, hiding her from being discovered.

She additionally personifies the knife, again suggesting that it will not be her who does the killing, that the knife itself will be the guilty one. The reference to 'heaven peeping' insinuates that heaven is somehow weak: there is no strength in peeping - it is the sort of thing nervous people do.

This binary between heaven and hell, with hell clearly winning on this occasion, is one that dominated the historical period, so the audience would fully understand what Lady Macbeth was alluding to.

I would hope by now you could see all the good stuff going on here. The candidate takes their analysis as far as they can, building one sentence on another.

2. USE PUNCTUATION CLEVERLY TO INDICATE YOU ARE ABOUT TO ANALYSE

This one is super easy to do but very effective. Use a colon (:) or dash (-) to show that you are about to analyse. You can see both of these in the passage above - check them out. You begin by placing the quote in context, then explore your ideas after the mark of punctuation:

'Thick' in this context refers to the night being unfeeling: by personifying night she seems to suggest that the night becomes an accomplice in her crime, hiding her from being discovered.

The reference to 'heaven peeping' insinuates that heaven is somehow weak: there is no strength in peeping - it is the sort of thing nervous people do.

3. USE SPECIFIC LANGUAGE TO SHOW YOU ARE ANALYSING

As I mentioned in an earlier section, I refer to these as analytical signposts. They are an easy way to say to the examiner 'hey, look what I'm doing, I'm analysing, please give me a higher grade'.

These are some good phrases to use:

This suggests…

This shows us…

This refers to…

The writer seems to suggest…

This insinuates…

You can see a number of these in the answer above.

4. USE AS BROAD A VOCABULARY AS POSSIBLE BUT KEEP IT CLEAR: DON'T DISAPPEAR UP YOUR OWN BACKSIDE

Sounds painful? Imagine an examiner having to read countless essays that are trying to sound clever but end up making no sense. Keep your writing clear and precise, but don't be afraid to use as broad a vocabulary as possible: examples above include 'accomplice', 'alluding' and 'binary'.

5. USE PHRASES TO SHOW POTENTIALLY DIFFERENT READINGS OF THE SAME QUOTE

This will take you into the 8s and 9s. Don't just settle for one analysis, think about how quotes can be read in different ways. You can use these phrases to signpost that you are examining alternative points of view:

One the other hand,

Conversely,

However,

One reading could be…. but another suggests….

Remember that different people can read texts in different ways: how we read Macbeth would differ hugely from how someone in the early 17th Century would have read it. If you're exploring things like the difference between male and female you could certainly refer to a modern reading in opposition to how someone in the 17th Century would have interpreted it.

SUMMING ANALYSIS UP

As you can see, analysing is really about four things:

1. Working out what the question is asking you to do;
2. Finding short quotes that answer the question;
3. Explaining how the quotes answer the question;
4. Using specific linking words and phrases to move the essay along.

It's number 3 where the magic is built, but it can't occur without the foundation of good quotes and the cement of those linking words.

Like every element of your exam, it really is all about practise. Follow my approach above until you know it by heart, then apply it logically in the exam. This will really help with exam nerves, as being able to revert to a simple process should give you some structure when your head's spinning.

8

OVER TO YOU...

To practise analysis, you need to head over to your exam board's website and download sample papers. You should practise both Language and Literature questions.

Here are the main exam boards' web addresses. If you're reading the print version just put the name of the board into Google and follow the links to GCSE and then English:

AQA: https://www.aqa.org.uk/subjects/english/gcse

Edexcel: https://qualifications.pearson.com/en/qualifications/edexcel-gcses.html

WJEC https://www.wjec.co.uk/qualifications/

OCR: https://www.ocr.org.uk/subjects/english/

CIE: https://www.cambridgeinternational.org/programmes-and-qualifications/cambridge-upper-secondary/cambridge-igcse/subjects/

9

A WORD ON WRITING UNDER PRESSURE

You've revised as much as you could, your bedroom a sea of post-it notes and index cards. You go into the exam quietly confident that you'll come out the other side intact.

You open the paper. Read the first question. No worries. Second and third, not too bad at all. The fourth is a little more challenging but that's ok, you've plenty of time. Two hours for this exam? Piece of cake. You'll be done with plenty of time to spare. What's the big deal?

With thirty minutes to spare you think you've finished. Turning idly through the paper just to see if you've missed anything, you suddenly realise there's a section B...

If I had a pound for every student who came out of the exam white-faced not having finished the exam paper, I'd not have to write any more books. (I'm glad that's not the case as I love writing them!)

These students (not from my class, I hasten to add) made the fatal mistake of either not reading the front of the paper well enough (if at all) or simply not timing themselves properly.

This final chapter is about just this. How to write under pressure so you maximise your chance at the highest marks.

Here are a few rules you should follow:

1. Do some maths to work out how many minutes per mark

Look at the number of marks the exam paper has in total, and look at the number of minutes you have for the entire exam. Divide minutes by marks to tell you how many minutes you should spend per mark, and therefore per question.

Say your exam is 2 hours long and is worth a total of 120 marks. That's pretty simple: it's about one minute per mark (120 marks, 120 minutes…). A 4 mark answer should therefore take no more than 4-5 minutes, whereas the larger 20 mark answer should take, you guessed it, around 20 minutes.

I would strongly suggest, as part of your revision, that you look at past papers and work this out in advance. It's not always exactly one minute per mark, but as the marks per question tend not to vary year to year you should know before you go into the exam roughly how long you should be spending on each question.

2. Be aware that the first few questions in a language exam are the lowest scoring, so get through them quickly.

Questions 1 and 2 in Language exams tend to be only worth a few marks. So spend as little time as possible on them. Focus your attention on the analysis questions as this is where you can make the biggest impression.

3. Write out a paragraph plan beforehand.

This one is hard to enforce, as students under pressure tend to just make it up as they go along. I don't advise this: even just a few words jotted down to remind you of what you should focus on per paragraph will keep you on track. You should in general be aiming to say one main thing per paragraph: your paragraphs don't have to be very long. What's most important is that what you say is super clear and logically laid out.

4. Remember that you're not expected to write a ten page essay in a one hour exam.

In fact, I would strongly advise against this. 1-2 sides of your answer paper for the longest Language questions and a couple of sides for Literature is more than enough to get you high marks. Think of the poor examiner, with five hundred exam scripts to mark. They're more likely to give you a high grade if you write two neat, logical and thoughtful sides than five sides of scribble.

5. Try to leave yourself five minutes to read it through.

I've mentioned this before because I have some vague hope that one day, someone I teach will actually do this. Maybe that person will be you? Who knows. But in all seriousness, it is such a useful thing to do.

You wouldn't think I'd publish this book without going through it line by line, looking for any tiny mistake and correcting it? Your exam isn't quite in the same league but spending a few minutes making sure it makes sense is a good idea.

6. Make sure you practise writing these essays under timed conditions as part of revision.

You may even want to ask someone in your family to invigilate so you feel under pressure. If you can practise working under the pressure of time you won't find it as daunting when you're in the exam room, as you'll know how long it takes to read the paper, find quotes, plan, and so on.

10

THANK YOU FOR READING

THAT'S IT FROM ME! I hope you find this little guide useful. If so, please leave me a review on Amazon: they make all the difference and mean that more people are likely to benefit from my years of experience and crazy desire to help as many of you as possible.

Please do also check out my other titles if they're of interest: more will be added soon.

AQA English Language GCSE 9-1 Revision Guide

AQA GCSE Macbeth Revision Guide

GCSE Inspector Calls Revision Guide

Best of luck - and just remember to breathe...

Printed in Great Britain
by Amazon

77529000R00058